The Book of Slime

To my dear friend Lowell Dabbs.
E.J.

Library of Congress Cataloging-in-Publication Data
Jackson, Ellen B., 1943–
The book of slime / by Ellen Jackson ; illustrated by Jan Davey Ellis.
p. cm.
Includes bibliographical references (p.   )
Summary: Describes some animals and plants that are slimy and
includes recipes for edible slime, slime jokes, and a slimy short story.
ISBN 0-7613-0042-2 (lib. bdg.)
1. Mucus—Juvenile literature. [1. Body fluids. 2. Mucus.]
I. Ellis, Jan Davey, ill. II. Title.
QP215.J33 1997
611'.0187—dc20   96-12831   CIP   AC
Published by The Millbrook Press, Inc.
2 Old New Milford Road, Brookfield, Connecticut 06804

The Book of Slime

by Ellen Jackson
illustrated by Jan Davey Ellis

The Millbrook Press
Brookfield, Connecticut

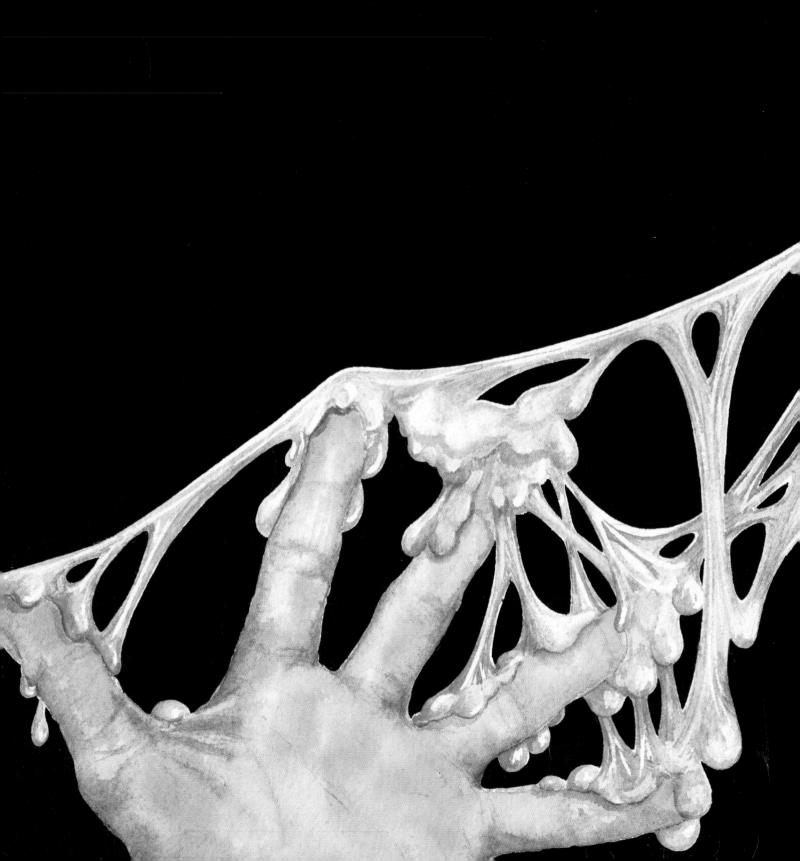

Slime is slippery. Slime is squirmy. Slime is anything that is oily, greasy, goopy, and gross.

Slime can be muddy and mucky. Slime can be old and moldy, and filled with grimy gunk.

Slime looks disgusting and yucky. But slime can be useful to animals and people.

The Slimy Facts

Do you want to feel nature's slime? Touch a wet fish, an oyster, or the white of a raw egg.

If you hold a raw egg in your hand, you will notice that the egg white feels like slimy goo. That's because it is made of water and protein. The egg white helps protect the yolk from banging or breaking against the shell.

Frog eggs do not have hard shells like the eggs in your refrigerator. Instead, they have a slimy coating that allows the eggs to stick to plants in a pond or stream. The sun warms the eggs while the young frogs are growing inside.

Snails have soft, slimy bodies. They slide along on a layer of ooze. The oozy slime keeps them safe from bumps and lumps on the ground.

Snails can glide up a pane of glass or move across a ceiling because their slime fixes them to the surface. They can even travel across a razor's edge on their cushion of slime without being cut.

Snails come out mostly at night or in damp weather because their skin dries out in the direct sunlight. You may have seen gleaming, silvery snail trails on the sidewalk after a spring rain.

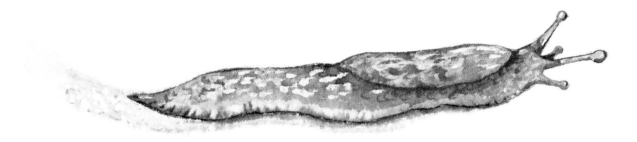

You may not want to cuddle with a snail, but snails like to touch each other. Two snails that are getting ready to lay eggs do a mating dance. First they press their slimy bodies together, then they touch each other with their eye stalks. Finally they exchange sperm. Then each wanders away to lay its eggs. (Unlike most animals, each snail has both male and female organs.)

Slugs are closely related to snails. They, too, are slimy, but they have no shells. If a snail is frightened, it pulls into its shell and seals the opening with a plug so it doesn't dry out. But if a slug is frightened, it curls up into a ball.

The hagfish is a true slimebag. It has so many slime glands that it can turn a bucket of water into a bucket of white slime in one minute.

You wouldn't want to meet this creature on a dark night. The hagfish bores into other fish and eats them from the inside out until nothing is left but a sack of skin and bones.

hagfish meets water....

.....hagfish slimes water

Eels make lots of slime if they are frightened or startled. They coat their skin with mucus until they are almost impossible to hold. This helps them escape from an enemy that might be interested in a tasty meal of eel.

In addition to animals, microscopic plants can be slimy to touch as well. Rocks in damp places are sometimes covered with slime from algae, a plantlike material with no leaves or roots. Lakes and ponds that are coated with algae have a slimy, scummy surface.

Have you noticed green gunk on the sides of your aquarium? That green gunk is algae. People often keep snails in aquariums because they eat the green algae, sucking green slime off the glass like little vacuum cleaners.

The Aztec Indians, who lived in Mexico hundreds of years ago, used to eat the slimy green algae that floated on the surface of Lake Texcoco. The Aztecs scooped it up in fine mesh nets. Then they dried it in the sun, shaped it into loaves, and ate it. Dried slime was said to taste like salty cheese.

Like animals, people have a slimy side to them—the inside, that is. Most of a person's insides are wet and slippery. In fact, about half of you is nothing but water.

Your tongue, your throat, and other parts of your body are slippery with saliva and mucus. Saliva helps you swish food around in your mouth and carry it to the back of your throat to be swallowed. Then it helps the food slide down your throat. Imagine trying to talk, sing, or whistle with no saliva to keep your mouth moist.

Saliva, or spit, comes out of salivary glands in your mouth and is made of water, mucus, and chemicals to help you digest your food. If you think about chocolate ice cream, or something else good to eat, your mouth will start making saliva about twenty times as fast as it usually does.

Your body makes about a quart (almost a liter) of saliva a day. That means an average person will make enough saliva during his or her lifetime to fill a bathtub 150 times.

Slimy Jokes

1. Why are monsters big, green, and slimy?
Answer: Because if they were small, black, and hard, they'd be marbles.

2. Why did the slimy monster enter the beauty contest?
Answer: To get some ooze and ahs.

3. Who won the slimy monster beauty contest?
Answer: No one.

4. Boy: "Hey. Bet you can't eat this green slime."
Girl: "Sure I can. I'm just waiting till it's ripe."

5. What's black and white and green all over?
Answer: A zebra that's been slimed.

6. Why didn't the sheriff put the slimeball in jail?
Answer: He was afraid it would give him the slip.

7. Chicks say, "Cheep! Cheep!"
Kittens say, "Mew! Mew!"
What do baby slugs say?
Answer: "Goo! Goo!"

How to Make Slime Nature's Way

Here is how to make your very own slime. Take a piece of tomato, a mushroom, a few leaves of lettuce, or a flower. Seal in a plastic bag along with a few drops of water. Store in a warm place for a week. Then open. The contents will be disgustingly slimy and smelly.

A Recipe for Edible Green Slime

You will need:

1 14-ounce can of sweetened condensed milk
1 tablespoon cornstarch
10-15 drops of green food coloring

Pour the condensed milk into a saucepan. Add the cornstarch and cook over low heat, stirring constantly. When the mixture thickens, remove from the heat and add the food coloring. Cool.

   This slime can be eaten or used as finger paint. Dip cooked noodles in it to make edible worms. Scare your brother and impress your friends!

Slime Pie

You will need:

a double portion of Green Slime
1 cup lime juice
8-ounce carton of whipping cream
graham cracker piecrust
1 package gummy worms

Mix up the edible green slime. Add lime juice to the mixture. Cook over low heat, stirring constantly. Add the food coloring. Whip the cream. Fold whipped cream into green slime mixture. Pour into graham cracker piecrust. Decorate with gummy worms. Freeze for 2 hours before serving.

A Slimy Story

Morris liked to put frogs down other kids' T-shirts. He liked to stomp on worms. He liked to put slugs in the blender and make strawberry slug-shakes.

One day, while playing in the alley, Morris saw a jar of green powder in a nearby trash can.

"Mix with water," read the directions on the jar.

Morris sprinkled a few grains of the powder into a bucket of water. The water hissed and sizzled. It burbled and bubbled. Soon the bucket was full of green slime.

"Wow!" said Morris. "I'm gonna have fun with this!"

The next morning, Morris put a glob of slime in his father's coffee. He giggled when he saw his father's green mustache.

He put another glob in his sister's sneakers.

"Maaa!" shrieked his sister.

But Morris's mom was busy cleaning up the mess the green slime had made in the microwave when it exploded.

At school, Morris slimed the pencil sharpener, the toilet seat in the boys' bathroom, and the teacher's cup of noodles.

He had so much fun that he dumped the rest of the powder in the bucket as soon as he got home from school.

Late that night, a smelly green mush burbled out of the bucket. It spread across the rug, eating Morris's books and tapes as it went.

"Burp!" said the slimy mush as it swallowed Morris's roller skates. Morris woke up to find a big pus-green monster standing over him slobbering and licking its chops.

"AAAAH!" screeched Morris as the monster oozed over him.

"Oh my aching tummy!" said the monster falling into Morris's bed. "I shouldn't have eaten those roller skates."

In the morning when Morris's parents went to wake him, all they could find was a puddle of green gunk lying in their son's bed.

Now they knew, once and for all, that their dear Morris really *was* a slimeball.

Bibliography

Buholzer, Theres. *Life of the Snail*. Minneapolis: Carolrhoda, 1985.

Cobb, Vicki. *Gobs of Goo*. New York: J.B. Lippincott, 1983.

Halton, Cheryl Mays. *Those Amazing Eels*. Minneapolis: Dillon Press, 1990.

Hanson, Jeanne K. *Your Amazing Body*. New York: W.H. Freeman, 1994.

Johnston, Ginny. *Slippery Babies*. New York: Morrow Junior Books, 1991.

Kellin, Sally Moffet. *A Book of Snails*. New York: Young Scott Books, 1968.

Little, Jocelyn. *World's Strangest Animal Facts*. New York: Sterling Publishing Company, 1995.

Rood, Ronald. *Who Wakes the Groundhog?* New York: W.W. Norton, 1973.

Thomson, Ruth. *Creepy Crawlies*. New York: Aladdin Books, 1990.

About the Author and Artist

Ellen Jackson is the author of a number of popular picture books, among them *Brown Cow, Green Grass, Yellow Mellow Sun* and *Cinder Edna.* Her earlier Millbrook title, *The Winter Solstice,* also illustrated by Jan Ellis, was named a Children's Choice book by the International Reading Association and The Children's Book Council. Ms. Jackson lives in Santa Barbara, California.

Jan Ellis has illustrated a number of popular Millbrook titles, among them *Mush! Across Alaska in the World's Longest Sled-Dog Race, Fiesta! Mexico's Great Celebrations, The Quilt Block History Of Pioneer Days,* and *Toad Overload: A True Tale of Nature Knocked Off Balance In Australia*. A resident of Columbus, Ohio, Ms. Ellis works with interior designers creating murals and hand-painted furniture.

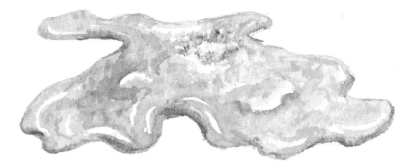